Creative Connections
and the Art of Play in the Music Classroom

Jane Barbe

Alfred Music
P.O. Box 10003
Van Nuys, CA 91410-0003
alfred.com

© 2014 by Alfred Music
All rights reserved. Printed in USA.
ISBN-10: 1-4706-1660-2
ISBN-13: 978-1-4706-1660-1

Table of Contents

Preface

Creative Connections compiles lessons, games, and strategies that are specially crafted to actively connect new material to prior knowledge. The activities utilize the art of play as a means of introducing, exploring, reviewing, applying, transferring, mastering, and assessing musical concepts.

The activities offer ideas for inexpensive yet creative manipulatives, such as large boxes and small, wooden rhythmic dice, beat boards, rhythmic-value-sized rhythm cards, stuffed animals, small play tents, and a giant, floor music staff. Also included are templates and visuals for immediate use in the classroom.

Additionally, these activities lend themselves well to meeting the *National Standard for Music Education*, as well as incorporating Common Core and professional growth evaluation goals, such as Marzano's "using physical movement" and "using academic games."

"Since the beginning of time, children have not loved to study. They would much rather play, and if you have their interests at heart, you will let them learn while they play; they will find that what they have mastered is child's play."
　　　—Carl Orff

"Play is the highest form of research."
　　　—Albert Einstein

"Children learn as they play. Most importantly, in play children learn how to learn."
　　　—O. Fred Donaldson

"Play is the work of a child."
　　　—Maria Montessori

"Play gives children a chance to practice what they are learning."
　　　—Mr. Rogers

"Play is often talked about as if it were a relief from serious learning. But for children, play is serious learning. Play is the work of children."
　　　—Fred Rogers

The Use of Transition Activities

Transition interludes are very useful for classroom management and opportunities for student involvement.

- For schools that have limited instrumentation, transition rhymes keep the students engaged, while providing each student with the opportunity to play an instrument.
- Transition activities give every student an opportunity to play instruments that are less commonly used in instrumentations, such as contra bass bars.
- Requiring students to speak the transition rhyme ensures that they will be actively engaged by limiting the amount of time between repetitions of the activity.

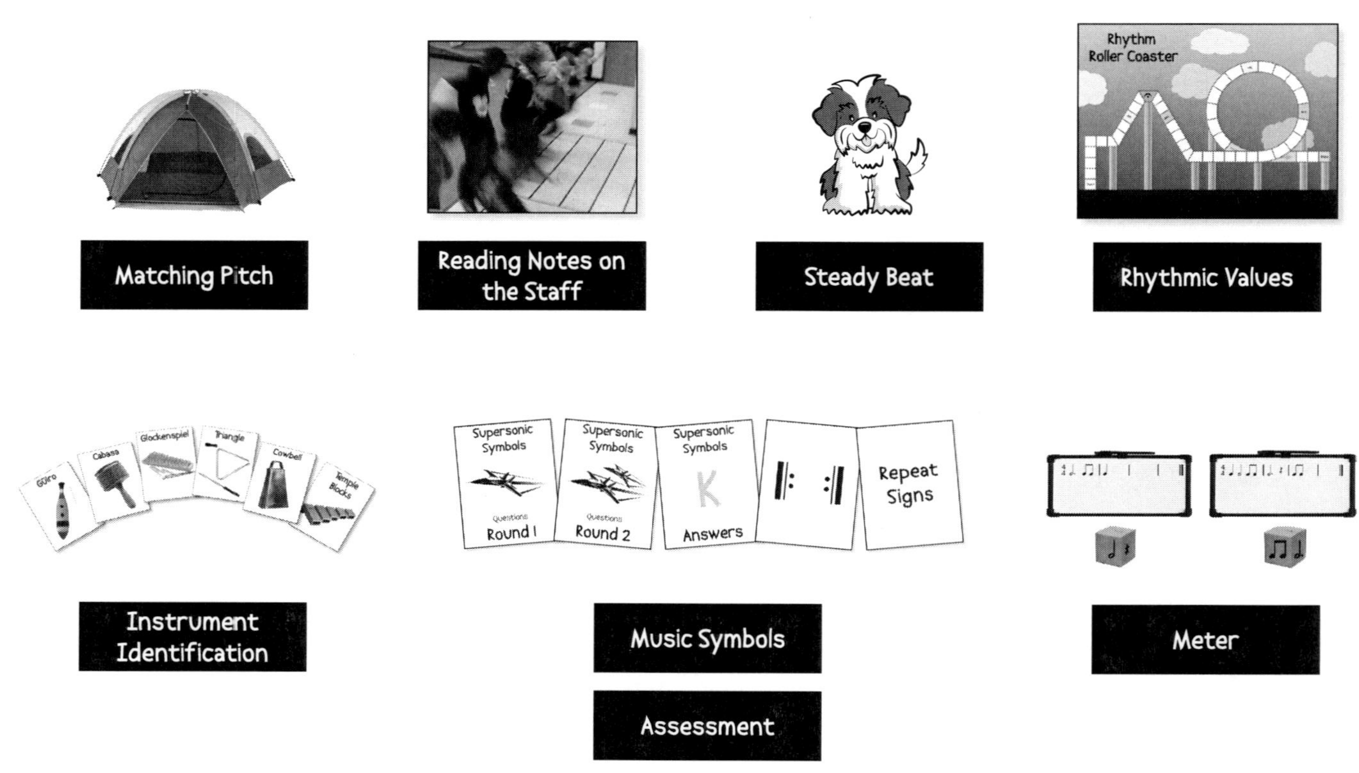

Reading Music in Any Clef With Just One Question: What Is the Bottom Line?

The process presented in this book was developed to remedy common misconceptions and misunderstandings involved with reading notes on the staff. Using **mnemonics**, the process includes teaching the staff as a staircase, the music alphabet, and students asking one question in order to read any notes in any clef. This has been found to help students:

- Read notes above and below the staff.
- Read in multiple clefs without memorizing multiple mnemonics. This is particularly important for students who play band and orchestra instruments.

Modern Mixer II

Hand Jive

P = Pat   L = Left
C = Clap   T = Together with Partner
R = Right

Cumulative Movements

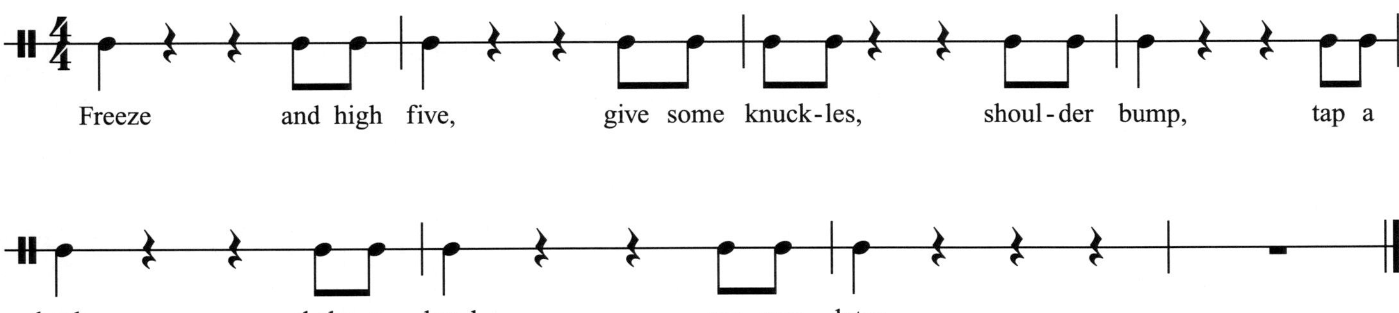

Interlude

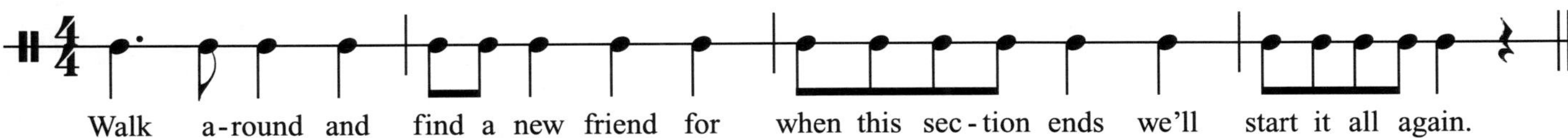

Form

- Song
- Interlude
- Song with one additional cumulative movement ("and high five")
- Interlude
- Song with first and second cumulative movements ("and high five"—"give some knuckles")
- The form continues until all cumulative movements have been performed.

Note: Due to the cumulative movements, an instrumental transition must be given by the teacher (♩ ♩ ♫ ♩) to clearly lead the students back into the next repetition of the song. Begin this rhythm, on the last word of the cumulative movements.

Process

- Engage students before they enter the room.
  - » With music playing, silently motion for students to follow you into a circle and to patschen the beat. The music should have a strong sense of pulse.
  - » As soon as the students are in place, have them join you in other beat-keeping movements, which change every phrase. Depending on the grade level, the movements may be as simple as patschen, clapping, or stepping in place, or as complex as body percussion patterns (Pat–Clap; Stomp–Pat–Clap; or Pat–Clap–Snap Right–Snap Left).
- As soon as the music ends, transition immediately into the Stomp–Clap movements of "Modern Mixer II."
- Utilizing silent directions often effectively increases student focus.
- Layer in the cumulative motions two beats at a time. State, "I am going to add something. Please tell me what I add and where to add it." (Stomp–Clap, Stomp–Clap–Stomp–Stomp–Clap, Stomp–Clap–Stomp–Stomp–Clap–Stomp–Clap–Freeze)
- Once the students perform the pattern accurately, add the corresponding lyrics (Stomp, Clap, etc.)
- Sing "Modern Mixer II," and state, "I am going to sing the song. Please raise your hand when you hear the part that we just learned."
- Sing the song, and cue the students to join in when the Stomp–Clap part occurs.
- Sing once again, teaching the hand jive movements that correspond with the first two phrases of the song.
- Once the song is secure, ask, "What do you think we are going to do with the hand jive movements?" (Answer: Perform them with a partner.)
- State, "Great idea! By the count of 20, please find a partner, and sit silently facing each other."
- State, model, and ask leading questions to make sure that the expectations are clear: "How much time do you have? What will you do when you find your partner? How will you sit? Great—here are your 20 seconds, 19, 18..." As soon as the first set of partners sit quietly, positively reinforce them to set a precedent for the class. "Wow, Johnny and Jane sat right away, and are facing each other silently. Great job!"
- Allowing the students guided and partner practice time, walk the students through the process for performing the hand jive with their partners. Make sure they pay special attention to starting with the pat on the word "hey."
- Perform the song and cumulative movements in their entirety with one partner. State, "You will know the song is over when we sing the words 'See you later.' Now, let us sing and move together."

- After the performance, ask, "What do you think we should do when we say, 'See you later?'" (Students answer: We will find a new partner.) Say, "That is a great idea. Let us learn a rhyme to help us pick a partner in time."
- Teach the interlude.
- State: "We are now ready to perform the entire mixer. We will begin with just the first movement: Freeze. Each time we travel to a new partner, we will add the next cumulative movement, until all have been performed.

Variations

Encourage the students to be creative with this experience. You can suggest that they:

- Strike a pose on Freeze.
- Perform with one partner instead of as a mixer.
- Perform with one movement per verse instead of as cumulative movements.

Dreaming

Syllabification to Rhythm
Drumming
Rhythm Composition
Rondo Performance

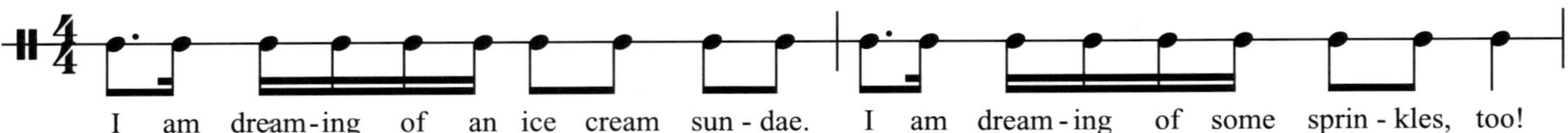

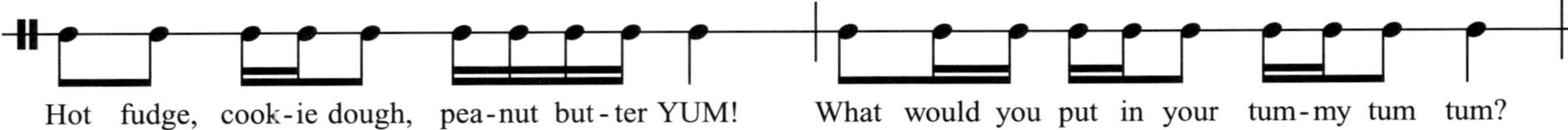

Alternate Lyrics

I am dreaming of an ice cream sundae.
Two scoops, whip cream, and a cherry, too.
Hot Fudge, Cookie Dough, Peanut Butter, Stop!
Pile it high but don't let it drop.

Drumming Process

- Teach the rhyme by rote or by having the students read the rhythm, incorporating the words once the rhythm is secure.
- Patsch the entire rhyme on the thighs with fingers spread slightly apart and relaxed.
- Cue the class to think the rhyme silently while saying only the words in ovals out loud.
- While thinking the rhyme silently, patsch only the words in ovals (the bass tones) by bouncing off the knee with the palm of the hand.
- Give the students guided and individual practice time to put the tones and bass tones together, again in body percussion. (Bass tones are represented by ovals and are performed with the palm on the knee. All other words are tones that are performed with relaxed fingers, slightly apart, on the thigh.)

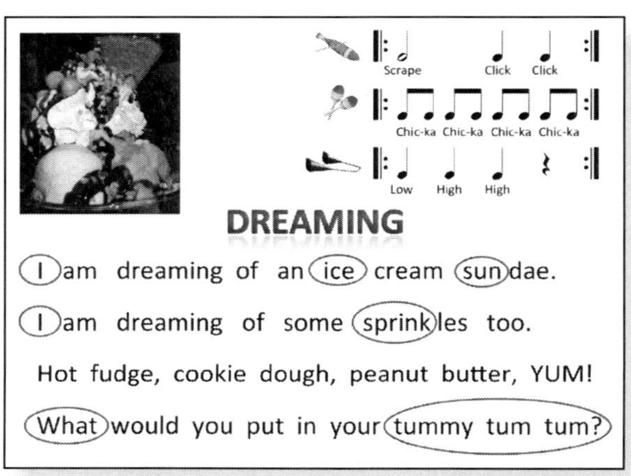

- Distribute drums with the following expectation: "When you get your drum, please put it down and place your hands in your lap. We will call this cue 'Drums Down–Hands in Lap.'"
- Play the entire rhyme on the edge of the drum. The fingers should be relaxed and spread slightly apart. Use the fingers just up to where they bend and meet the hand.
- Play only the words in ovals. Make sure the fleshy part of the palm bounces off the center of the drum.
- Give the students time to practice putting together the tones and the bass notes.
- Perform the entire rhyme.
- Teach unpitched instrument patterns using words and movements.
  - » Scrape – slide hand down opposite arm
  - » Click – karate chop move on wrist of same arm
  - » Chicka – patsch alternating right and left hands on thighs
  - » Low – tap wrist of opposite wrist
  - » High – tap shoulder of same arm
- To make sure that the rhythms fit together properly, say the rhyme while the students say and move unpitched parts.
- Once all the parts are secure, divide the class into four groups, and rotate who says each part (including the rhyme).
- Perform all the parts together, in a circular set-up so that each student has an opportunity to play each instrument. This avoids the statement: "I've been here since kindergarten. Now I'm in fifth grade, and I have never played the contra bass bars."

Drum	Agogô Bell
Agogô Bell	Drum
Drum	Agogô Bell
Agogô Bell	Drum
Drum	Maracas
Agogô Bell	Drum
Drum	Maracas
Guiro	Drum
Drum	Maracas
Guiro	Drum

Rhythmic Composition

- Divide the class into small groups.
- Make sure each group receives one "beat board" and one packet of eight "toppings": three quarter notes, two eighth notes, one sixteenth note, and one of each division of the sixteenth note.

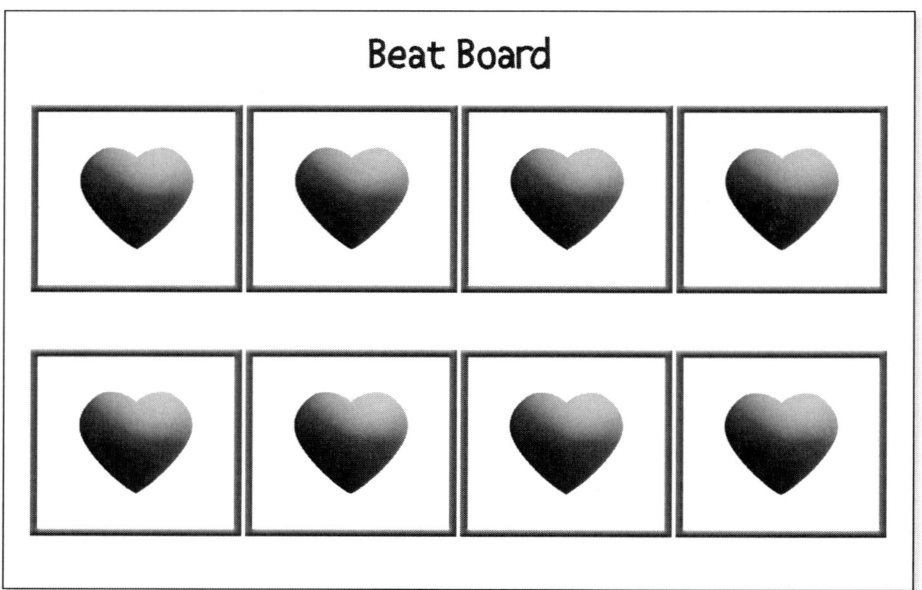

- Have the groups arrange the toppings so that one picture is placed on each heart (or in each box).
- Provide a beat anchor on a hand drum as the students speak their pattern. This will help the students think in terms of sounds per beat.
- Give students time to evaluate and adjust their patterns, if necessary.

Rhythm Identification

- Give students rhythm cards and time to determine the rhythm of each topping. The rhythms should be aligned above the first row of toppings and below the second row so that they can see both the rhythm and its corresponding topping.

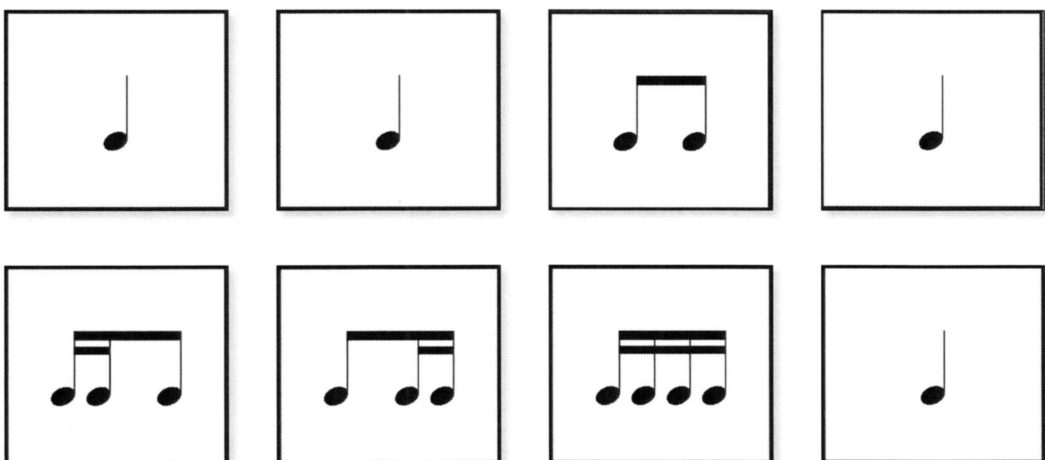

- **Common Core Extension:** Have students work in groups to identify the fractional relationship of the sounds per beat for every rhythm (e.g., an eighth, two-sixteenths pattern fractionally equals ½, ¼, ¼).
- Additional Identification Options:
  - » Cooperative group discussion and matching.
  - » Class Cooperative Discussion and Matching: "Who has a word that has one syllable?"
  - » Whiteboards (Melamine) or Socks:
    - − Write rhythms on the board.
    - − Make a list on the board.
  - » Velcroing rhythm cards under pictures.

Unpitched Instruments

- Let the students choose unpitched instruments to play their patterns.
- Encourage students to be creative with their instrument choices. Pose the following questions:
  - » Will you use different timbres for different rhythms?
  - » Will every person in your group play the entire rhythmic pattern?
  - » Will you each play a different rhythm?
  - » What other creative ideas can you come up with to play your pattern?

Performance

- **Rondo:** Perform in rondo form with half the class playing the drumming rhyme as the A section and half of the small groups performing their compositions as the subsequent sections.
- Have each group say their topping pattern once and then play the pattern on their unpitched instruments. This sixteen-beat pattern will align the rondo sections with the A-section melody.
- Switch groups performing the drumming with the small group compositions and perform once again.

In the Hall of the Mountain King

Process

- Begin class with a rhythmic reaction game:
  - » Walk the quarter notes, accompanied by a hand drum.
  - » Slide the half notes to the sound of a triangle.
  - » Tiptoe the eighth notes to temple blocks.
- Give the students a visual of the rhythmic pattern; have the students speak and clap, whisper and clap, and internalize and clap the rhythmic pattern.
- Instruct the students to clap only on the quarter notes and internalize the remaining rhythms.
- Have the students add the eighth notes as tiptoes, followed by half notes (tied quarters), with a firework motion.
- Students sit and listen to "In the Hall of the Mountain King" by Edvard Grieg, with the following focus question: "Why would I have you stop performing the movement to listen to this music?"
- Play the music until the beginning of the *accelerando*.
- The students should identify the rhythm as the one from the visual.
- Transfer the tied quarter notes to the traditional half-note symbol, as reflected by the change on the visual.
- Ask, "Why would I have used two quarter notes, tied together, instead of the half-note symbol? (Answer: "So that we could see that it equals two quarter notes.")
- Have the students perform movements with the recording, up to the *accelerando*.

- Once their performance is secure, and without prior knowledge of the end of the piece, students perform the entire piece. They typically have a lot of fun trying to keep up with the music.

- Discuss the *accelerando*, the subsequent *crescendo*, and the rhythmic variations.

- Have the students perform the piece once again, after advising: "This will be challenging by the end, but I know that you can do it! Concentrate on performing each quarter note in time."

- Conclude with a rhythmic math problem. Ask students to determine the rhythmic values for each letter below.

Variations

- Instead of using movement to represent each rhythmic value, substitute unpitched instruments. This variation provides a great opportunity to discuss instruments that are best used for longer notes, such as a triangle for a half note, versus a drum or woodblock for eighth notes.

- Provide the students with a picture of a troll or a boy on a tongue depressor stick to keep the beat throughout the song on a tempo board. This will help them experience the *accelerando*.

Tip

- When handing out small instruments or other materials, give them to one student to pass the items around the circle, one at a time. When the student to the right of the "passer" receives an item, instruct that student to place it on the floor and place hands in the lap. These motions alert the person to the "receiver's" right that he or she will receive the next item. This process continues until each student has obtained an item.

Rhythm Roller Coaster

Materials

- Whiteboard
- Markers
- Colored Beads (used as game pieces)
- Wooden Cubes/Dice with grade-level-appropriate rhythms written on the sides

Game Board

- Using the whiteboard, create a game board with squares in the shape of a roller coaster.
- The strategic squares should include pitfalls and forward-moving musical terms:
  » Rit. (*Ritardando*): Go back one space.
  » Acc. (*Accelerando*): Go forward one space.
  » ⌢ (*Fermata*): Lose a turn.
  » Other musically creative squares.

Directions

- Divide the class into small groups, and direct the students to place their beads on the START square.
- Instruct the students to take turns rolling the die. The rhythm rolled determines the number of squares that the student will move each turn.
- The student who reaches the FINE square first wins the game.

Beat Box

The students must have prior knowledge of meter, bar lines, and rhythmic values.

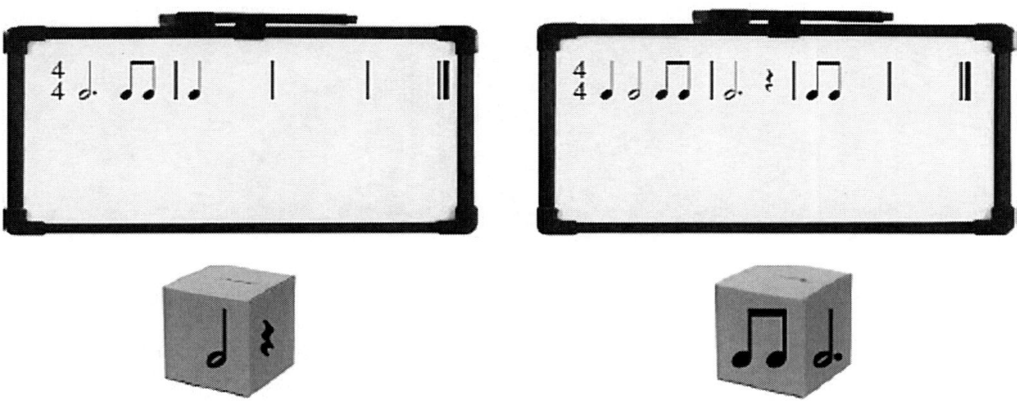

Big Box Rhythmic Dice

Formation

- Set up two whiteboards, or a smartboard, with four measures, a grade-level-appropriate time signature, and a double bar line.
- Divide the class into two or three teams, each with their own whiteboard, or place on a smartboard. The teams do not have to be equal.
- Have one team line up in relay-race fashion behind each whiteboard.
- Present one Big Box Die to each team with grade-level-appropriate rhythms written on each side.

Process

- As a relay, each student rolls the die and determines whether the rhythm rolled fits into the measure, according to what previous students have written.
- If the rhythm rolled does fit in the current measure, the student writes it onto the board.
- If it does not fit, the student must state, "This does not fit," and proceed to the end of the line without writing anything.
- Measures must be written in order.
- The first team to accurately complete their four measures, according to the time signature, and to acknowledge the double bar line as "the end," earns the point for that round.
- Note: This game can be played with any grade-level-appropriate rhythms on the die and in any time signature. $\frac{6}{8}$ time works particularly well with $\frac{6}{8}$ rhythms on the die. The rhythmic values are doubled from what the students know of $\frac{4}{4}$, $\frac{2}{4}$, and $\frac{3}{4}$ time.

Who's Hiding in the Tent?

Concepts

Matching Pitch

Vocal Timbre

Assessment

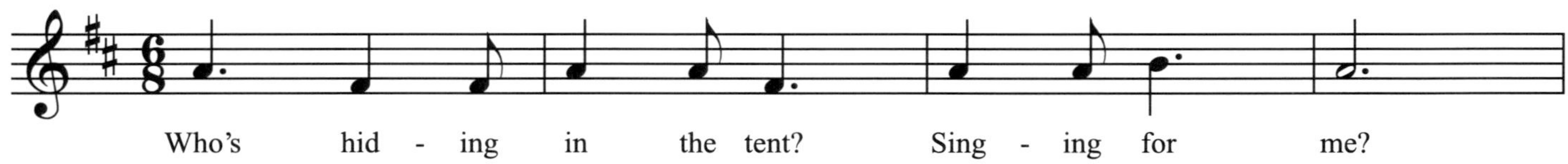

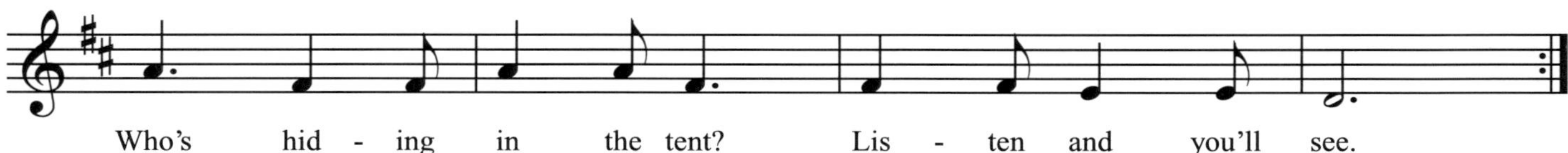

Call and Response

Teacher Call

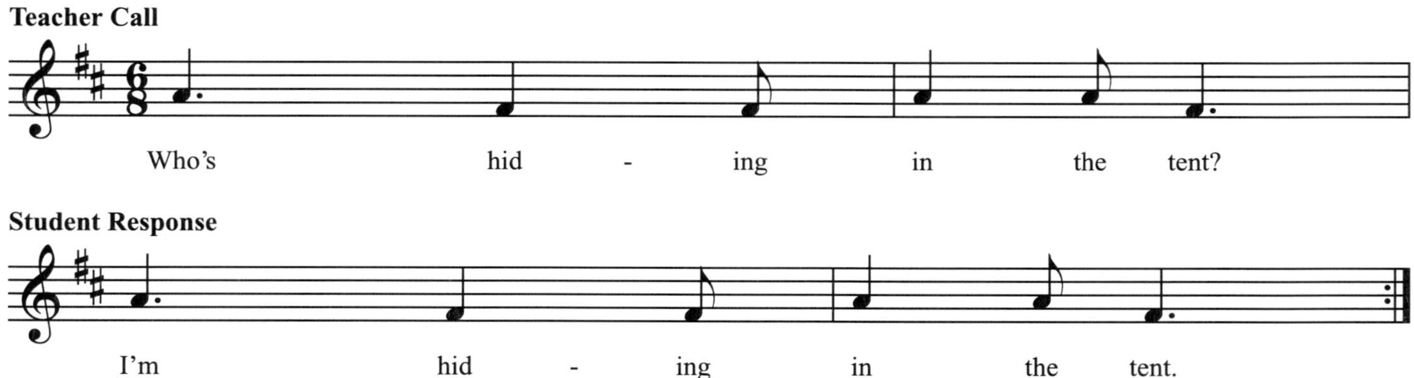

Student Response

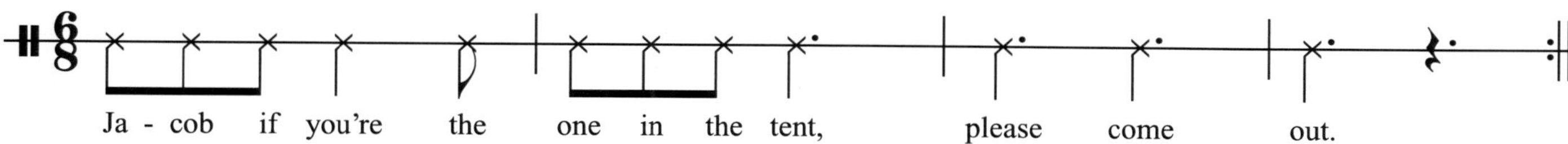

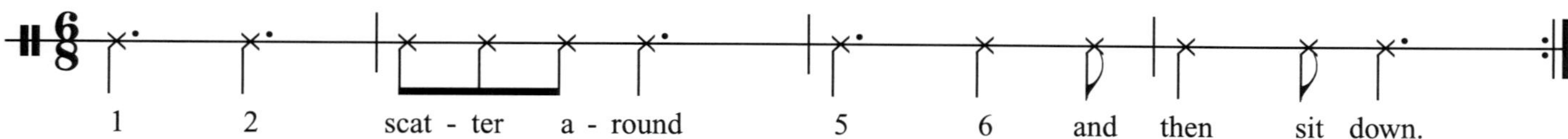

Rotation Game

Formation

- Instruct the students to sit in a scattered formation. They may sit within the typical sitting area, but make sure they are not in a circle and not by instruments.

Form

- Song
- Call and Response
- Identification
- Interlude

Process

- Teach the song by phrase.
- Have the students close their eyes and sing the song. As they do, tap a student on the shoulder to go hide inside the tent.
- Have the class sing the call and the student in the tent sing the response.
- Have the class identify the student with the Identification Pattern.
- Speak and play the scramble rhyme while all the students quickly find a new spot to sit. This step makes it more difficult to identify who is missing.
- Students repeat the song while the student who was in the tent chooses another student to hide.
- The game continues in the same manner.

Assessment

Objective: The student consistently matches pitch while singing a short melodic solo.

Rubric:

5 Consistently matches pitch with musicality.

4 Consistently matches pitch.

3 Consistently sings above or below pitch.

2 Consistently speaks or chants.

1 Does not attempt the activity.

Extension

After students have completed their turn in the tent, they rotate through a line of accompaniment parts. Grade level appropriate modifications, to the accompaniment and call and response, may be made to contour to the needs of the students.

Process

- Present the following visual:

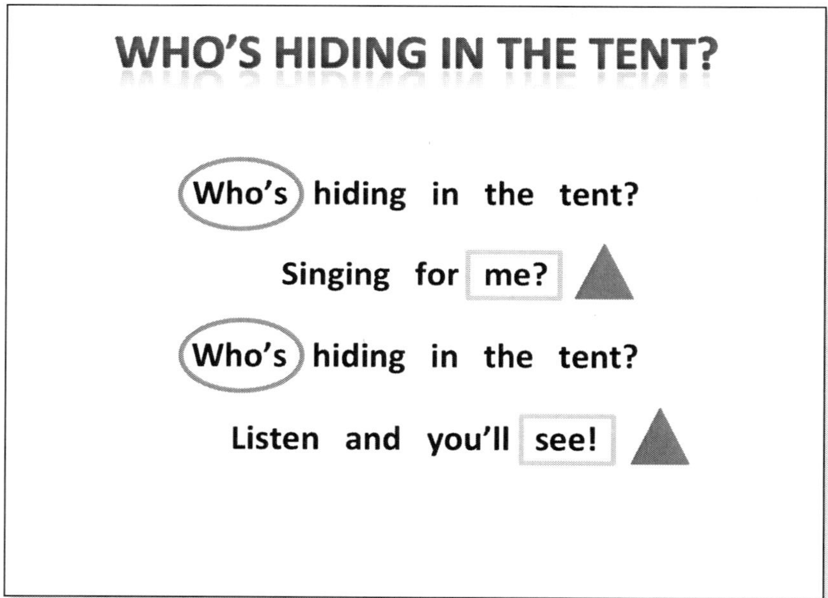

- State, "I am going to add something to the song. Please tell me what I add and where to add it."
- Sing the song while clapping on the word "who's."
- Have the students identify the new part as claps on the words that have ovals.
- Have the students perform the song with the claps.
- Follow the same process of asking the students to identify the rectangles as patsching.
- Have students perform the song with the ovals and rectangles.

- Have students identify the triangles as snaps and perform with all three body percussion moves.
- Teach the bass xylophone part using the line, "Who's that, hiding there?" patching on knees.
- Add the contra bass part as a stomp.
- Divide the class into sections.
    - » Have the sections play each part together.
    - » Rotate the parts, until each group has experienced each instrumental part.
    - » Instruct the students to move to instruments set up in pentatonic.
    - » The class practices each part on whatever instrument they are on at the time.
- When each part has been experienced, have the students return to the original formation for the game. Arrange one of every instrument in the instrumentation in a row in front of the tent: contra bass bar, bass xylophone, alto metallophone, and soprano glockenspiel.
- After a student has had a turn in the tent, he or she should go to the first instrument in the row and work through all the parts on each subsequent repetition of the game. After finishing, they return to their seats.
- **Additional Option:** The rotation instrumentation may be taught during the game, with each part presented as the first person exiting the tent arrives at each subsequent instrument, in order from lowest to highest.

Notes

- For younger students, remove unnecessary bars from the instruments, leaving only the bars that will be played for each part.
- If Orff instruments are not available, the following substitutions may be made:
    - » triangle, soprano glockenspiel
    - » finger cymbals, alto metallophone
    - » woodblock/temple blocks or bass xylophone
    - » drum, contra bass bar

Who's Hiding in the Tent? – Instrumentation

Listen Up!

Concepts

Instrument Timbre

Identifying Instruments by Sound

Process

- Teach the song by phrase.
- State, "I am going to add something to the song. Please tell me what I add and where to add it."
- Have the students identify the claps as the ovals on the visual.

- Have students perform the song with the claps.
- Note: There are primary and secondary clapping patterns.
- Introduce the tent and encourage discussion about each instrument that will be placed in it. For clear identification of instruments within an instrument family, focus on what type of sound it makes rather than the material it is made of. For example, metals ring, woods knock, brass instruments all make their sound by buzzing into a mouthpiece, and woodwind instruments make their sound by blowing into them.
- Demonstrate playing an instrument inside the tent, and have students discover that the oval claps will be where the instrument is played during the game.
- Students are chosen to go into the tent, one at a time, to play an instrument of their choice.
- Ask the class, small groups, or individual students to name the instrument played.

Identification

- Position large boxes near the tent, with pictures or names of instruments on each side. Ask each student to identify the instrument heard using the boxes.
- Provide all the students with one instrument and have them respond by playing, only if they have the same instrument or an instrument that is in the same family as the one they heard.
- Provide students with packets of instrument pictures. Cue them to close their eyes and hold up the instrument picture that matches the instrument played.
- Provide the students with packets of instrument names.
- Each student has a single instrument picture, which should be raised when the instrument is heard.
- Provide the students with a worksheet containing a line of small instrument pictures next to a numbered example. Students should circle the instrument that is played by each student in turn.
- Create your own ideas, or ask your students for theirs!

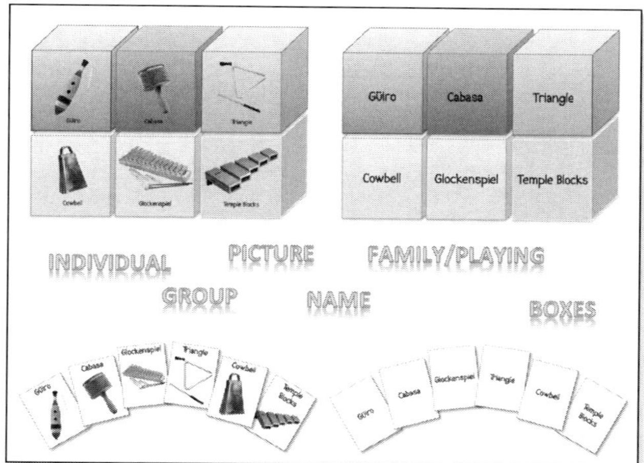

Assessment

Objective: Students will identify instrument sounds.

Rubric:

- **4** The student accurately identifies 3 of 3 instruments.
- **3** The student accurately identifies 2 of 3 instruments.
- **2** The student accurately identifies 1 of 3 instruments.
- **1** The students does not identify any of the instruments.

The Little Old Lady Who Was Not Afraid of Anything

(From *The Little Old Lady Who Was Not Afraid of Anything* by Linda D. Williams)

Process

- Read the book to the students, and draw out the line, "But behind her, she could hear two shoes go . . . "
- Once each object has been introduced, students finish the sentence for the teacher.
- Teach the song.
- Introduce pre-selected instruments such as hand drums, maracas, tambourine, etc. Include instruments that would make sense for the knock on the door and the sound of the rocking chair.
- Discuss each instrument's sound, concentrating on the sound it produces rather than its material.
- Have the students choose which instruments best match each sound described in the book.
- Introduce props: boots, pants, a shirt, a hat, gloves, and a pumpkin head (to be carried, not worn).
- Divide the class in half to perform the movement with props and to play the instruments.
- Repeat the performance so that the teams may switch.

The Little Old Lady Who Was Not Afraid of Anything — Instrumentation

- Present the following visual:

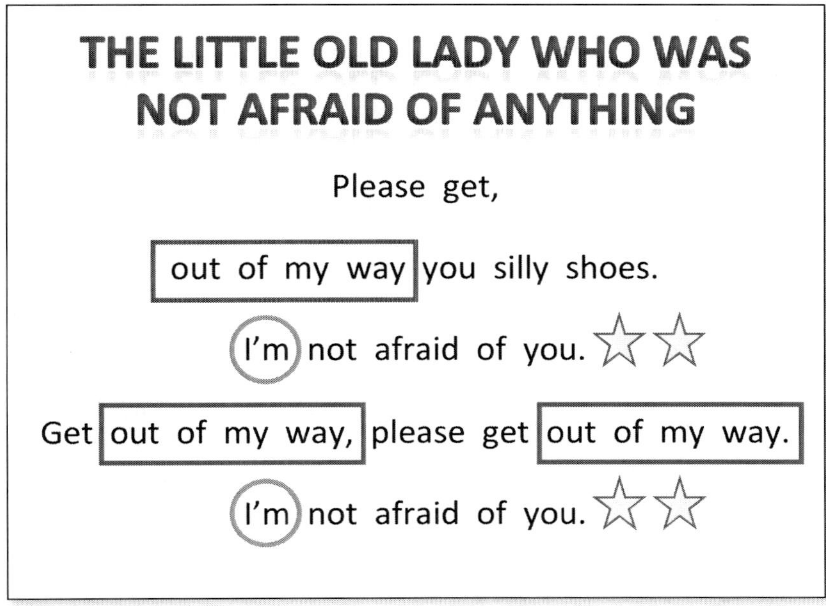

- State, "I am going to add something. Please tell me what I add and where to add it."
  - » Introduce "out of my way" in patschen.
  - » Ask the students to identify the movement, pat, where it occurs, "out of my way," and the rectangle presentation on the visual.
  - » Transfer and play the parts on an alto xylophone until the students have learned them as body percussion.
- Pose the statement again, and use the same process for the following parts:
  - » Circle "I'm," clap, soprano metallophone
  - » Stars, snap, soprano and/or alto glockenspiel
  - » Stomp, contra bass bar
- With each new part, divide the class in two so that each side experiences two parts simultaneously. Then do the same for three parts.
- Introduce the bass xylophone part, which the player should play for the duration of the performance.
- Assign different instruments to the students so that each part is played.
- Add a cymbal jazz pattern if appropriate for the level of students.

Pete the Cat: I Love My White Shoes

(*Pete the Cat: I Love My White Shoes* by James Dean and Eric Litwin)

Process

- Read the book, posing questions to the students about the color the shoes would turn.
- Students speak the lines "Oh, no!" and "Goodness, no!" where they occur in the story.
- Teach the song.
- Ask the students to identify and place the basic melodic contour cards in order.

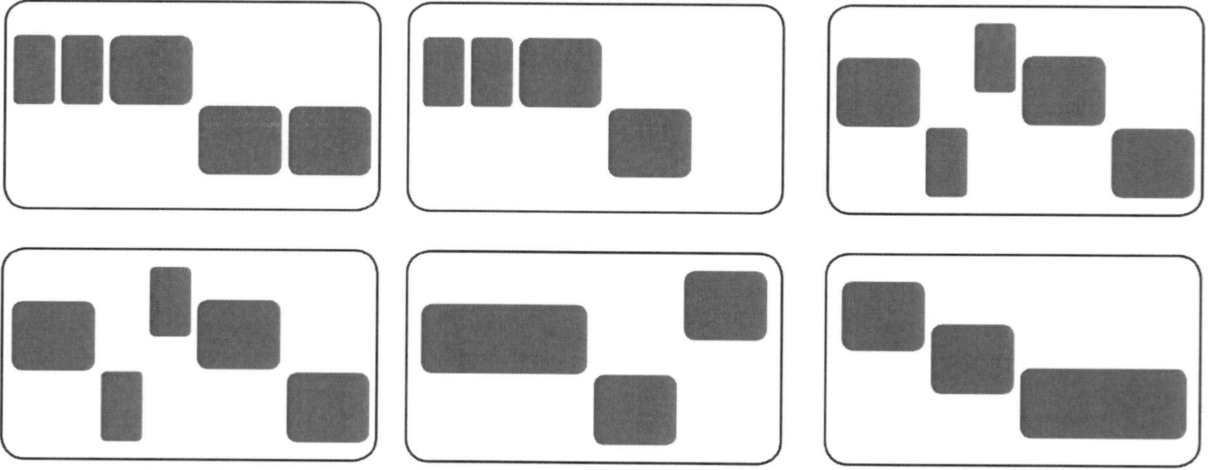

- You may choose to add a seventh card that does not fit in the song to avoid the process of elimination.
- Read the book with the performance of the song, changing the colors as they occur in the story.
- Presenting cards that spell the color correctly but are in the wrong colored fonts are a good way evaluate the students' reading skills.

Alphabet Rap and Word Jump

Materials

Floor Staff

Process

- The floor staff is a tool to learn the notes on a staff, instead of using memorization. The students often do not learn how to read notes above and below the staff, and they can confuse the lines for spaces or vice versa. This method also prevents them from being able to transfer their knowledge between clefs.

- Teach the musical alphabet to show that the staff works like a staircase.

- Present the students with two giant floor staves, created with painter's tape or chalk.

- Divide the class into two teams per staff, or four teams total. The teams do not have to be equal. Have the students line up, in straight lines, behind the staves.

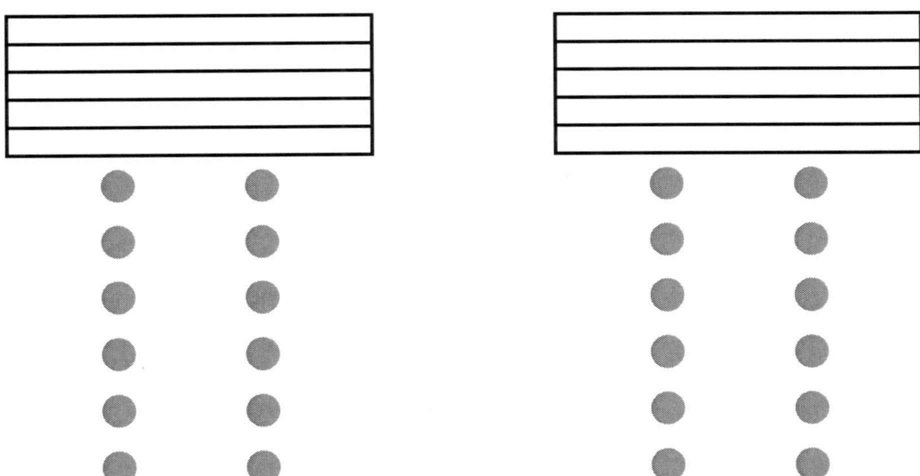

- Begin playing the beat on an unpitched instrument to anchor the movement and cue the first students on each team to walk the staff together. The entire class should simultaneously speak, "Line, space, line, space."

- Once they have completed their walk, immediately recite the transition rhyme.

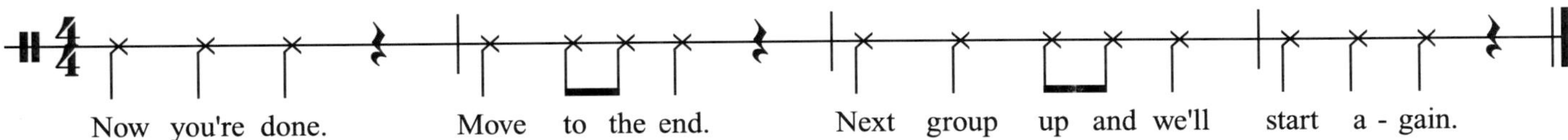

- When every student has completed a turn, introduce the musical alphabet with the following rap. The repetition of this rap is meant to elicit laughter and recognition that the musical alphabet only has seven letters.

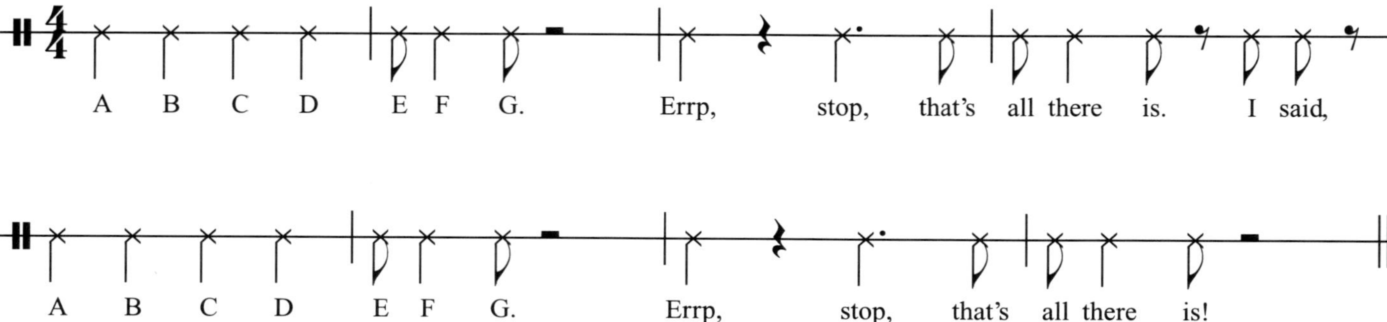

- State, "You will be able to read in any clef—treble clef, bass clef, and alto clef—right away using only one question: 'What is the bottom line?'"
- Present catch phrases. "Treble Clef is E, E, Easy."
- In time with your drum beat, the students will begin walking the staff while stating the treble clef phrase, followed by "Alphabet Rap." Once they complete the walk, they should once again use the transition rhyme.
- Introduce, "Bass Clef is G, G, Great, and Alto Clef is F, F, Fun." This will show the students that they can read any clef if they understand that the staff works as a staircase, use the musical alphabet, and know the bottom line.

Word Jump

- Using the giant floor staves, divide the class into teams of three or four students, who sit in an "open space" around the room (but close enough that they can all see).
- Bring the two teams up to the staves to compete.
- Each team lines up behind their own staff, with their toes touching the bottom line.
- Present the same word to both teams. (If a team has an extra player, you may double up one letter, or if a team does not have enough students, one letter may be omitted.)
- Make each student responsible for one letter in order of the spelling of the word. For example, the student on the far left of each team, facing the staff, would be responsible for the first letter; the person to their right is responsible for the second letter of the word and so forth.
- Give the students time to walk the staff and verbalize the "Alphabet" rhyme, in order to determine the placement of their letter.
- Students return to the start where their toes will once again touch the bottom line.
- Cue, "1, 2, 3, jump," so that the students jump or safely walk to their letters simultaneously, as in a race.
- The first team to accurately spell their word moves to the right-hand staff and challenges another team.
- Refer to the staff on the left as the challenger's side and the staff to the right as the champion's side.
- If students are in band and orchestra, they may use their clef to spell their word. For example, if students in one group play trombone, viola, flute, and violin, they can all jump to the line or space that represents the letter in their instruments' clef.

Puppy Dog

Interlude

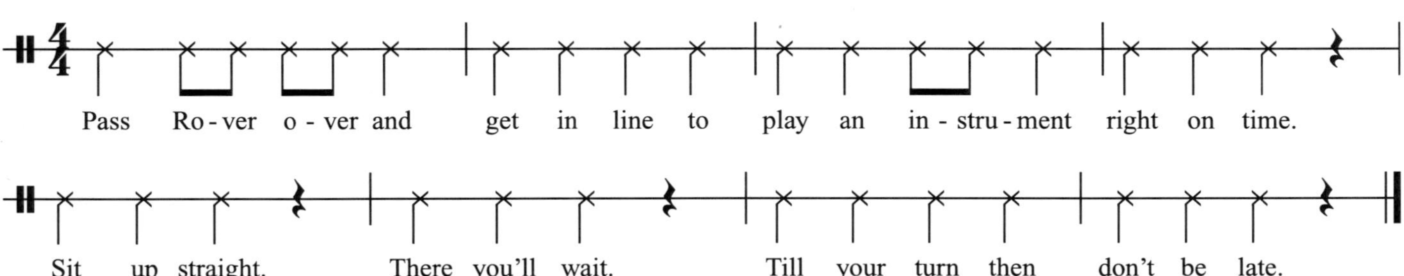

Rotation Game

Formation

Ask the students to form a circle. In the middle of the circle, place two carpet squares in a line to lead to a woodblock, xylophone, and/or contra bass bar.

Process

- Sing the song, and cue the students to patsch the beat.
- Teach the song by phrase.
- Introduce Rover, a stuffed puppy dog with beanbag feet, and demonstrate how to keep the beat with his paw.
- Perform the interlude, and silently hand Rover to a student.
- During subsequent repetitions, silently lead the students to pass Rover to a new student, proceed to the first carpet square to wait one round, and then play the beat on a pitched or unpitched instrument. Several instruments may be used in a rotation, including a woodblock, contra bass bar, and a bass xylophone with all the bars removed except for D and A.
- To peak interest and focus, the teacher may randomly choose students to take turns, instead of going around the circle. Giving one particularly well-behaved student a turn illustrates what you are expecting from the students.
- After playing the instrument, the student may return to his or her place in the circle for the rest of the game.

Four White Horses

Caribbean Folk Song

<table>
<tr><td>Concept</td></tr>
<tr><td>Steady Beat: Secondary</td></tr>
</table>

Transition

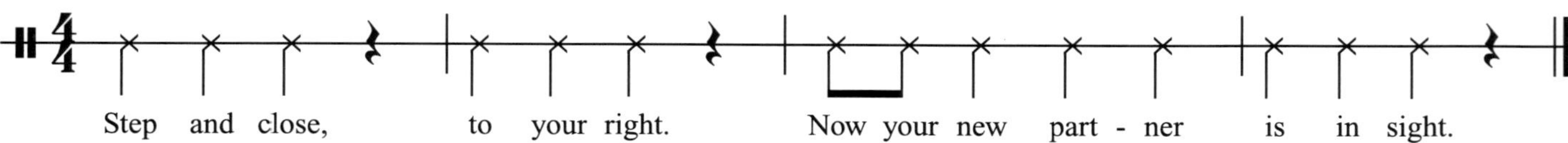

Formation

Have the students pair up and form concentric circles.

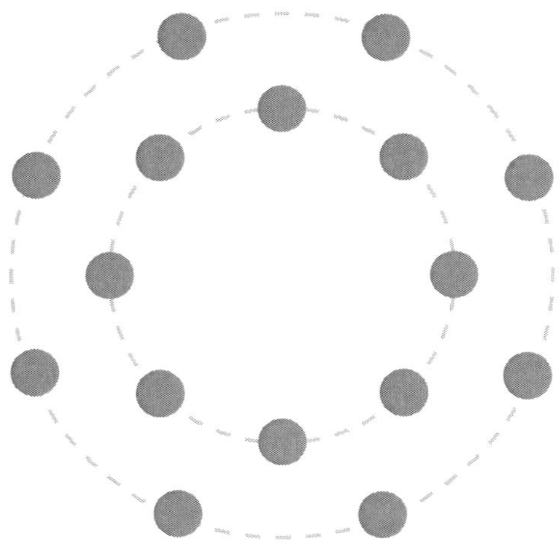

Process

- Silently teach students the hand jive: Pat, Clap, Right, Clap, Left.
- While anchoring the beat with a hand drum, have the students choose partners and practice the hand jive.
- Introduce the song.
- Perform the song with the hand jive.
- Introduce the interlude spoken by the teacher and the students.
- Note: Only the outside circle should move.
- Demonstrate how the inside circle of students will move one person to their right during the transition. Often, having the outside circle sit during this step is helpful for visual learners.
- Perform the song, followed by the transition, until the students are back to their original partners.

Tips

- This type of activity works with any nursery rhyme or hand jive game. Make sure the movements are grade-level appropriate to avoid poor coordination or hindering the students' ability to keep the beat.
- Require the students to say the interlude to prevent unwanted behavior.

The Syncopated Clock

By Leroy Anderson

Concepts

Rondo Form
Creative Movement
Listening

Formation

Divide the class into small groups, each with their "own space."

Process

- Ask the students to listen to the A section and brainstorm what they think the music is about.
- Explain music's ability to make you use your imagination and create your own story.
- Introduce Leroy Anderson and explain the concept of the grandfather clock in his piece "The Syncopated Clock."
- Divide the class into small groups and instruct them to create locomotor or non-locomotor movements that represent the A section.

Time, Energy, Space, and Levels

- Encourage students to be creative with their movement choices: Time, Energy, Space, and Levels.
- Pose open-ended questions:
  - » Should the entire group of students perform the exact same movements?
  - » Could the group join together to form a shape while they move?
  - » Should their formation include students at different levels (high, middle, and low)?
  - » Could some students perform one type of movement while others perform a complementary or contrasting movement?
- Allow time for the students to practice their movements with the music and make adjustments if necessary.
- Students perform their creative movement each time that they hear the A section. Instruct them to sit if anything other than the A section is heard.
- Play the entire piece for the students. Ask them to perform their movements when they hear the A section and to sit whenever it is not present.

- Draw the letter A on the board every time the students perform, and leave spaces to represent the times they are seated.
- Help students identify why they made the choice to sit during the listening activity. (The A melody went away.)
- Ask the students to identify the B section during the activity. They should deduce that the movements for this section should differ from those of the A section.
- Give students time to create movement for this section.
- Repeat this process for the C section.
- Once students have identified and created movements for the whole piece, display the form on the board as ABACA.

Rondo Rap

- Introduce or review rondo form with the following rhyme:

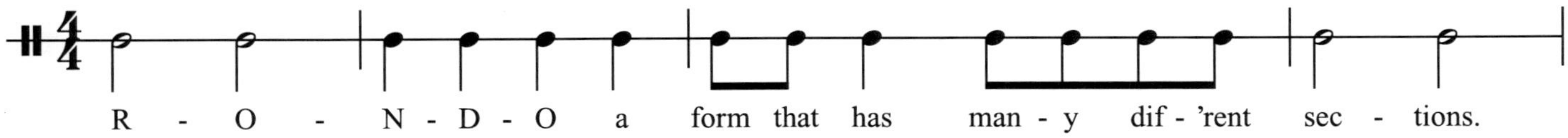

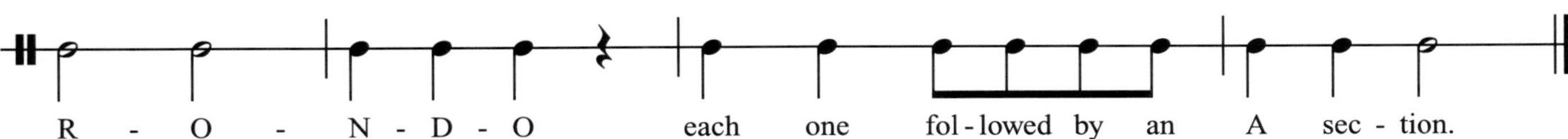

- Perform the entire song with movements.
- Have groups perform individually while others watch and provide positive feedback.
  - » Use a prompt such as, "I like how . . . "

Variations

- Perform the "Rondo Rap" as a song with instrumentation.
- Teach the instrumental parts with the words written in the score, until the parts are secure.

Rondo Rap – Instrumentation

Supersonic Symbols

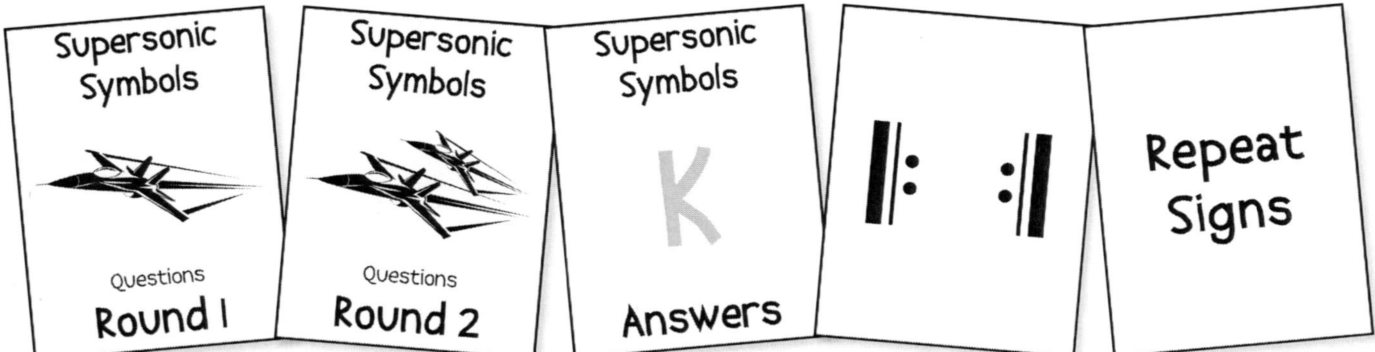

Materials

- Key Cards (marked on the back with a "K" so you know which ones they are after each round of the game)
- Round 1 Cards (marked with "R1" on the back of each card)
- Round 2 Cards (marked with "R2" on the back of each card)

Directions

- Each team will have one set of K, R1, and R2 cards that are all the same color. You will need enough sets in different colors to accommodate teams of five to ten students (red, orange, green, pink, purple, yellow, and blue).
- Divide the students into relay teams.
- Place a set of R1 cards in a neat pile face down (with the "R1" showing, but not the side with the questions).
- Have each team form a single-file line behind their R1 cards.
- Place the key cards in a messy pile, face up (with the definitions showing instead of the letter K). Have the students search through this pile to find the match to their R1 cards.
- Start the game by saying, "Go."
- Have the first student in each line pick up the card on top of their R1 pile and then proceed to the messy key card pile to find the matching card.
- When the correct match is found, the student presents the pair to the teacher.
- If the match is incorrect, respond with "Not yet—try again." Provide small hints as desired.
- If the match is correct, say, "Yes, that is correct." The student should then place the key card back in the messy pile and the R1 card in the discard pile, which is next to their R1 pile.
- The first team to complete their R1 pile receives a point.
- Give the other teams a chance to complete their R1 pile for half points before having the class move on to the R2 pile.
- The game may be played at the beginning and end of the year, or at the beginning and end of a unit, for evaluation purposes.

Term Mania

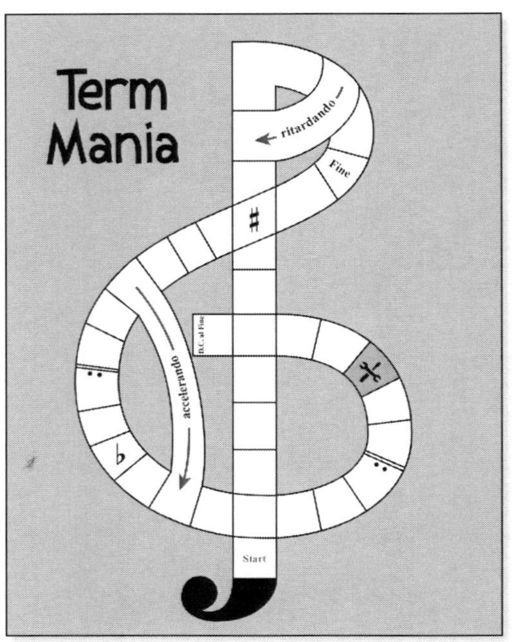

Materials

- Poster Board
- Markers
- Colored Beads
- Dice (Traditional)

Game Board

- Create the spaces in the form of a treble clef.
- The strategic squares should include grade-level appropriate pitfalls and forward-moving musical terms:
  - » *Instrument Repair Shop* – Lose a turn.
  - » Sharp (♯) – Move forward one space.
  - » Flat (♭) – Go back one space.
  - » *Accelerando* – Move forward, up the ladder.
  - » *D.C. al Fine* – Go back to the beginning and work your way to the *Fine*.
  - » ⫶| – Go back and find the other matching repeat sign(|⫶). Continue from that square.
  - » *Fine* – The first person to land on the *Fine* (after taking the *D.C. al Fine*) wins the game.

Coda: Assessment

What Is Assessment?

Assessment is simply documenting student progress.

At what level was the student at the beginning of the year?

Where is the student now?

Where should the student be?

Assessment is defined as documenting student progress. In the past, the standard method for assessment has been via paper and pencil, but it does not have to be! Since music is performance based, shouldn't a percentage of musical assessments be carried out through active music performance? Assessment can be as simple as observing a student keep the beat or respond to music. In addition, recording assessments does not have to be difficult or time consuming!

Assessment does not have to be an intimidating experience for students. When assessing young students, let them know that you will be observing them during an activity rather than telling them that they are having a "test." For example, see if they are "keeping the beat in time with the music." Make sure that they understand what mastery looks and sounds like as well as the rubric or assessment tool that is marking their progress. Utilizing manipulatives (such as blow-up microphones and tents) and/or assessing students individually (for example, while playing a game) take a great deal of pressure off them and allow them to perform their best.

Quality Assessments

Are the assessments:

- **reliable**, producing the same results with the same students each time, and
- **valid**, measuring what they are supposed to measure?

When to Assess?

- **Formative** assessment occurs during the learning process and provides information used for instructional purposes.
- **Summative** assessment occurs at the end of the learning unit.
- **Informal** assessment is for your information only and does not factor into grading.
- **Formal** assessment contributes to grades.

What to Assess?

This depends on what you are teaching the students (i.e. your district curriculum) or what you are teaching each grading period.

Types and Tools

Knowledge (Recalling)

- Fill in the Blank
- Matching
- Multiple Choice
- Recall Verbal Responses
- Musical Examples:
    » Relay races placing recorder fingerings with notes on the staff.
    » Naming notes on the staff. Matching notes on the staff.
    » Identifying instruments by sound.
    » Matching a French horn with its mouthpiece.
    » Matching a violin with its bow.
    » Matching a rhythm with its beat value.
    » Filling in the beat value of a rhythm.
    » Matching notes on the staff with their alphabet letter.

Skill (Performing)

Musical Examples:
- Reading and playing rhythmic patterns.
- Playing an instrument with proper technique.
- Matching a pitch vocally.
- Keeping the beat during a hand jive game.
- Keeping the beat on an instrument.

Product (Creating/Making)

Musical Examples:
- Create an ostinato (written).
- Place instrument pictures into the correct families on a poster.